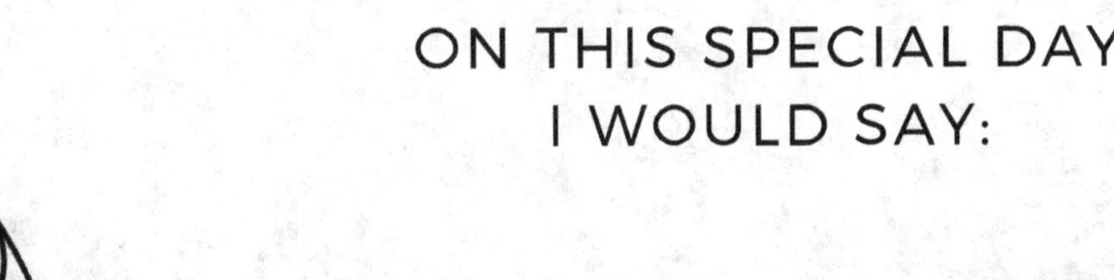

ON THIS SPECIAL DAY
I WOULD SAY:

THANKS
MOM

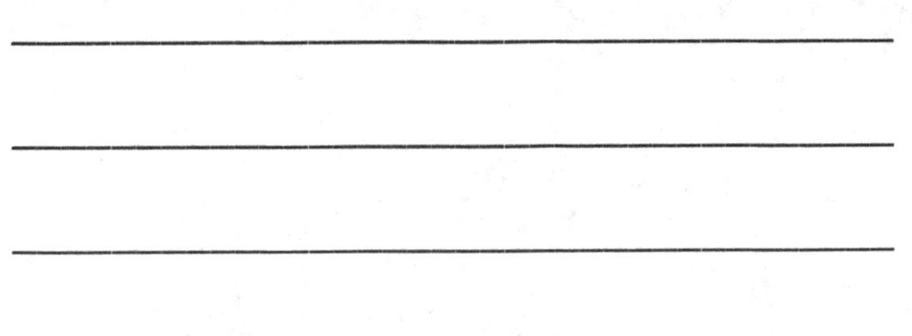

____

____

____

____

Thanks for
EXISTING
MOM

to my
SUPER
Mom

TO YOU WHO ARE
My Safe
HOME

TO MY FAVORITE
MOM

IN MY EVERY
BREATH
THERE IS A
PART OF YOU

THANKS FOR THE
sweetness
of your hugs

THANKS
MOM
FOR YOUR
PATIENCE

WOMAN
WIFE
MOM...
UNIQUE

My
HEART
is for
loving you

your day is
EVERY DAY
Mom

YOUR
HUGS
WARM
MY HEART

a hug for a
Lifetime

when you smile..
you Shine

to you who
choose with
LOVE

THE MOST T
DIFFICULT
and
BEATIFUL
job in the world

I wish your
wishes
come true

thank you
for making

THE MOST

whith the

RESOURCES

you had

to you who
gave me
LIFE

for all the
thanks
that I didn't say
to you at
the right time

with you I'm
not afraid
of anything..

The most
beatiful
Flower
Is the love
of the mom

Mom
the most beautiful
name in the
world

MOM
the first word
that enters
your heart

you and I
were born
together mom

even when you
are not there,
I feel you
CLOSE

the determination
of the mama is
UNBEATABLE

WITH YOU I HAVE
SPENT THE MOST
BEAUTIFUL DAYS
OF MY CHILDHOOD

your love
knows no
BOUNDS

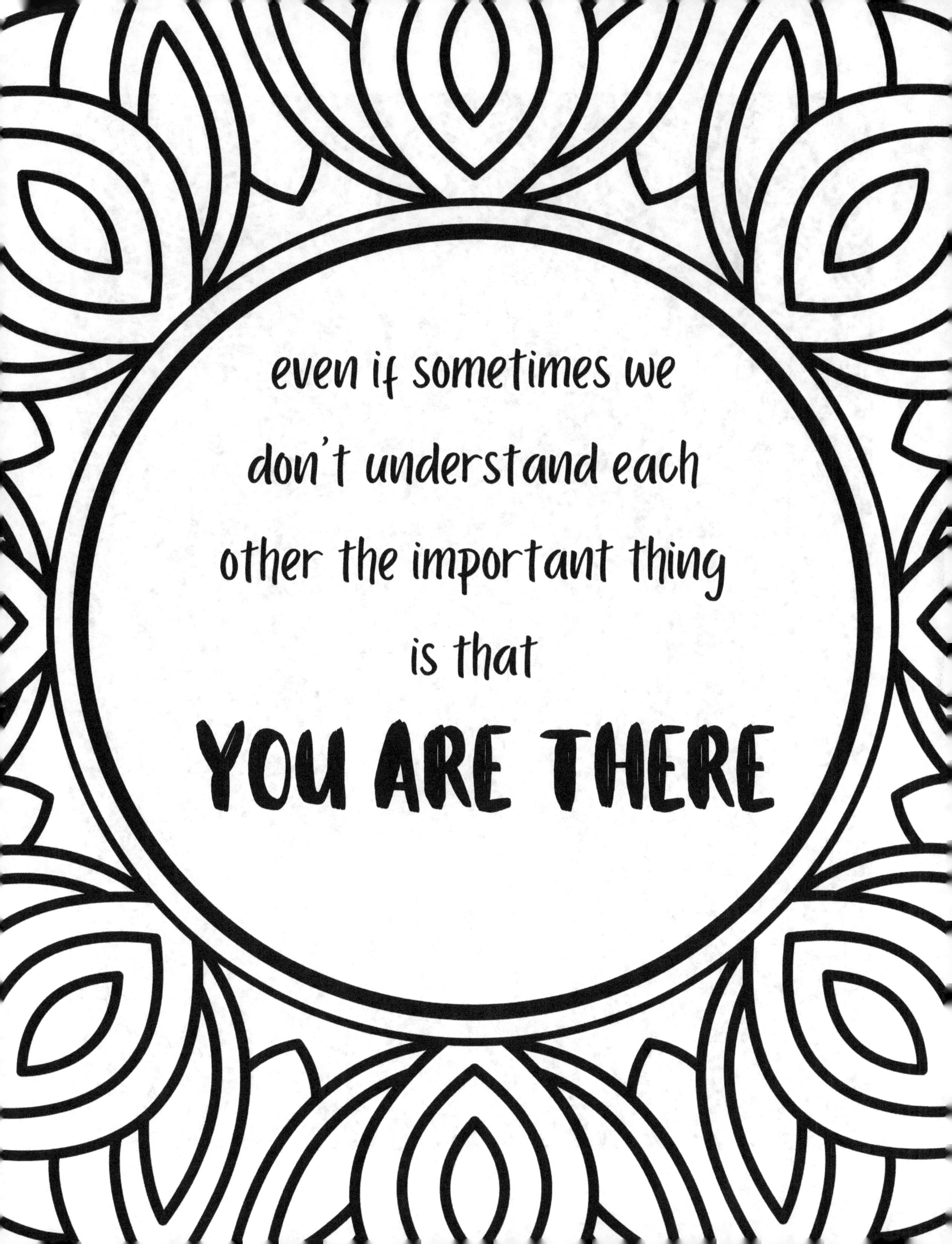

even if sometimes we
don't understand each
other the important thing
is that
YOU ARE THERE

to you who
read
my mind

to you who do
7 things
at the same timee

THANKS
FOR PUTTING
UP WITH ME EVEN
WHEN I DON'T
DESERVE IT

to you who have
SUPERHEARING

when i miss
you it's
BECAUSE I LOVE
YOU MOM

WHEN
YOU SUFFER
I SUFFER

YOU MAKE
ME HAPPY
MOM

WHATEVER
HAPPENS
YOU WILL HAVE ME
BY YOUR SIDE

YOU ARE
you want
you can do
EVERYTHING

you are
important
to me

MOM
is
FOREVER

I TRUST
YOU
MOM

THE IMPORTANT
THING IS NOT TO BE
PERFECT BUT
UNITED

to you who
owe my
LIFE

yesterday,
today,
tomorrow ..
IN MY HEART

to our
WONDER
WOMAN

my heart
will alwaysi
look for you
wherever
you are..

THANK YOU
MOM TO
YOU WHO HAVE
ALWAYS REMAINED
close to me